Coca-Cola®
Collectible
Polar Bears

THE OFFICIAL COCA-COLA COLLECTORS SERIES

Coca-Cola Collectible Bean Bags & Plush

Coca-Cola Collectible Cars & Trucks

Coca-Cola Collectible Polar Bears

Coca-Cola Collectible Santas

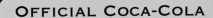

Coca-Cola®
Collectible
Polar Bears

LINDA LEE HARRY
JEAN GIBBS-SIMPSON

BECKETT PUBLICATIONS

Published by: Beckett Publications
15850 Dallas Parkway
Dallas, Texas 75248

ISBN: 1-887432-92-2
Beckett is a registered trademark of Beckett Publications

First Edition: September 2000
Beckett Corporate Sales and Information (972) 991-6657

The contributors to this publication have attempted to place current fair market value on each collectible. This book is to be used as a guide only. Prices in this guide reflect current retail rates determined just prior to printing. Prices are based on a grading system of 1–10 (with 10 being Mint and 1 being poor). As always, items are only worth what someone is willing to pay for them. Auction and dealer prices will vary based on condition, geographic location and demand. Neither the Authors nor the Publisher assumes responsibility for any losses that might be incurred through the sale or purchase of merchandise because of the information contained herein.

All items photographed for this book are in Mint condition, unless stated otherwise.

Printed in Canada

Contents

Foreword

By Jean Gibbs-Simpson

Who collects Coca-Cola polar bears, and why? The answer to the first part is easy: almost anybody. Because of the nature of our subject and the types of items that it adorns, I suspect more women and children collect the Coca-Cola polar bear than men. But plenty of guys sport the shirts, carry the cooler bags, hoard the collector and phone cards and acquire all the model cars, trucks, planes

and NASCAR pit stop scenes they can stuff into their homes. Certainly, Coca-Cola polar bear collectors represent the distant poles and everything in between, no matter their careers, ages, locations or financial status.

The "why" is much more complex, and I'm not sure that anyone can provide a single reason. In more than twenty-five years of dragging home anything I could afford that carried the logo of The Coca-Cola Company (from an empty movie popcorn box to a billboard), I've been asked "why?" lots of times. Collecting polar bears is just an extension of the same behavior, only there are more factors involved.

In this hobby (collecting Coke stuff),

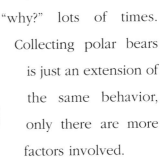

there are at least three types of buyers, the first a fairly new creature:

- A "day trader" finds a piece at an auction, garage sale, or even club meet, that is perceived to be worth more than the selling price. Within twenty-four hours, the item appears on the Internet and a profit is made. This is not the behavior of a true collector, unless this is a duplicate piece, but the transactions affect the market for collectors.

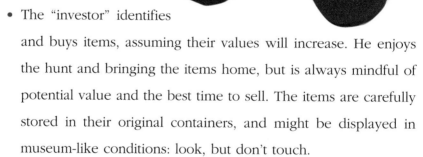

- The "investor" identifies and buys items, assuming their values will increase. He enjoys the hunt and bringing the items home, but is always mindful of potential value and the best time to sell. The items are carefully stored in their original containers, and might be displayed in museum-like conditions: look, but don't touch.

- A "real thing" collector—that's me—displays his treasures so that they can be touched and enjoyed, perhaps in every room in the house, basement and garage. This type of collector can recount stories about how pieces were acquired and loves to share them with anyone who can be dragged in for a guided tour. Oh, the collection will someday be sold if the kids don't want to inherit it. My children, having grown up around this obsession, wouldn't touch my collection for any price. But, in the meantime, it will be enjoyed, even on cleaning days.

People who collect Coca-Cola polar bears surely belong to the "real thing" category. Why else would someone part with anywhere from $5 to $50 for yet another bear item every few days when he knows there aren't two inches of display room left at home, that its value probably will not accrue and the piece looks awfully similar to two hundred other items already in residence?

Some people simply say, "Because I like them," or, "They make me feel good." As with the other-than-polar-bear portions of our Coca-Cola home decorations, other factors can come into play.

At the beginning, the treasure hunt aspect is the hook. You realize you can find the familiar red and white logo almost anywhere, whether new or antique. That opens up so many venues to search: auctions, flea markets, antique malls, gift shops, the Kmart/Wal-Mart/Target loop, garage sales, grocery stores, service stations and even trash deposited in front of strangers' homes. Yes, trash. One of the most gentle, refined ladies I've known used to carry trash sacks and boxes in the trunk of her luxury car so that she could "rescue" items as she drove around Atlanta. If she located something such as a Coke cooler or old bottle, she'd stop and ask the owners if she could have it. (A very desirable old piece needn't be in Mint condition.) And she's not the only person to enhance a collection that way.

But most people can't sustain that first rush of excitement forever. Eventually, you've visited and revisited all of the haunts located within a day's or weekend's drive. So how does the average Coca-Cola collector hang in there for twenty-five years? By making associations and forging lasting friendships during the journeys. The Coca-Cola Collectors Club, over six thousand members strong, is regarded as one big family, and each meet is a reunion. The organization recognizes fifty chapters throughout America, Canada, Europe, and Australia, and most chapters meet periodically and have a special event annually. There are many more Coca-Cola collectors not affiliated with the organization; they're just out there collecting all things Coke. That's

apparent when new items hit the market: available one day and gone the next. I am the only member of the club in my city of seventy-five thousand, but newly released Coke items disappear from store shelves, sometimes before I arrive. A recent auction contained only two Coke signs among the hundreds of things sold that day. It attracted at least a dozen people who stood around for several hours waiting for the crew to work around to that part of the room where the signs were displayed. I've come to know every one of those free spirits, even though they can't be talked into joining TCCCC.

My narrowing of focus from all Coca-Cola collectibles to mostly polar bears happened unconsciously. Not since the 1940s, when the Company introduced an impish character called Sprite Boy,

has the young-at-heart identified with such a lovable, grin-producing object.

Perhaps it is simply a continuation of the teddy bear popularity that has been with us since the early twentieth century. Many Coca-Cola polar bears go home with people who don't collect other items from the Company. These collectors, no doubt, are bitten by the nostalgia bug. Or perhaps they collect other bears, collector plates, car models, playing cards, etc., and the Coca-Cola editions fit right in.

The Sprite Boy, with his signature soda jerk or bottle cap hat, was featured on thousands of advertising pieces from the 1940s and '50s, and still appears on collectibles reproduced today. However, the sheer number of items carrying the Sprite Boy image doesn't come close to the thousands the polar bear has inspired.

Sprite Boy was printed on signs, school supplies, thermometers, grocery bag holders, bottle cartons, sporting event programs . . . not just items manufactured to be used around the house. Our furry friend has been used on just about every advertising piece possible.

Young consumers take bear-adorned items to school in a luncheon or

From Coca-Cola Polar Bear print advertisement

book-bag, wear them to play, cuddle with them in their bedroom or hang them on the wall. To avid adult bear fans, no function of everyday life is complete without a polar bear influence: an alarm clock, salt and pepper shakers, mugs, plates and silverware, a telephone, jewelry, purses, Christmas ornaments and even a throw for those cold nights in front of the TV. These things will be outgrown or will wear out. (Of course, there is probably a duplicate stored safely in the collection.)

Although many of these items are made to be consumed, there are pieces meant to be saved and displayed: collector figurines, plates, hanging art and plush bear with musical actions.

The irony of polar bears selling Coke around the world is that the decision makers who determine the next big advertising theme never envisioned how popular the bears would become, nor how long the love affair with the public would last. They are as amazed as the collectors,

and now there are no apparent plans for the animals to go into hibernation anytime in the near future. Plans for next season call for many more new bears, maybe even more than in past seasons. (Heaven help the checkbook.)

The bottom line is that Coca-Cola polar bears are attractive and inviting to all types of collectors. And, most of all, they're just plain fun.

Introduction

For the past century Coca-Cola has been a fixture in American life, progressing from a local soda fountain drink created by Atlanta pharmacist John Pemberton in 1886 to a worldwide soft drink empire.

To do so, The Coca-Cola Company has used virtually every conceivable promotional tool to advertise and sell its product. From bottles to signs, trays to calendars, novelties to toys, the images of Coca-Cola fill our lives and reflect our times.

Why are Coca-Cola collectibles so popular? "Coca-Cola" is the most-recognized trademark in the world. The name evokes images of happy times shared with family and friends.

The trademark "Coca-Cola" in its distinctive Spencerian script was first registered with the US Patent and Trademark Office in 1893.

Coca-Cola Collectors Club 1998 exclusive

"Coke" was first registered in 1945. The shape of the contour bottle, so distinct you could pick a bottle up in the dark and know it was "the real thing," was first registered as a trademark in April, 1960.

The Coca-Cola Company insists that every item carrying its trademarks be meticulously crafted to exacting standards. In recognition of this standard of excellence, millions of devoted collectors around the world snatch up anything and everything with that familiar "Coca-Cola" trademark. It could be argued that Coke collectors rank among the most loyal collectors anywhere.

Not that it took diehard allegiance for Coca-Cola enthusiasts to accept the polar bear. When the Company, already known for its creative marketing, introduced the polar bear in a 1993 television advertisement, one of the most successful ad campaigns—and a whole new category of collecting—was born.

The first commercial featured a community of polar bears kicking back and enjoying their favorite drink while watching the Northern Lights. Over-

night, the "Always Coca-Cola" Polar Bear became a dazzling superstar.

During the past several years, these friendly polar bears have appeared in six more popular advertisements. Their playful antics and charming animation elevated them to the status of global icon, recognized the world over.

The polar bear images, favorites with children and adults alike, appear on everything from plush toys and bean bags to figurines and Christmas ornaments. Coca-Cola collectors, and bear lovers, snap up these furry friends to fill their homes with some of the most broadly appealing product lines ever created.

Polar Bear Love Affair

A century ago, German toy maker Richard Steiff sketched an idea for a new toy after watching a troupe of performing bears in an American circus. His design for a standing bear, jointed similarly to a doll, began a new industry.

At the same time, President Theodore Roosevelt failed to find anything to shoot on a hunting trip in Mississippi. According

to reporters, aides found a lost bear cub and tied it to a tree, thinking this would serve as the president's trophy for the day. Upon seeing the defenseless cub, Roosevelt ordered it to be released.

A newspaper cartoon entitled "Drawing the line in Mississippi" recorded the event and captured a nation's heart. Brooklyn candy store owner Morris Michtom produced two "Teddy" bears to mark the occasion and the world's love affair with bears began.

The spark was rekindled with the debut of the Coca-Cola polar bears in 1993. The Coca-Cola Company has found the perfect four-legged promoter in the polar bear. His Arctic homeland reminds us that Coke is always best served "Ice Cold" while his playful antics symbolize fun and good times spent with family and friends. Likenesses of the famous

polar bears can be found everywhere to the delight of collectors worldwide.

Cast of Characters

The Adult Bear—its image has graced more products than any other bear around! Usually just its head and paw are seen in front of a blue Arctic backdrop. Easy to recognize, just look for his admiring gaze at an uplifted bottle of Coke. The "Always Coca-Cola" red disc icon is somewhere in the scene. The design of this famous bear is now a trademark.

When those playful cubs are on the loose, the adult bear is never far behind! Most collectors assume when an adult bear is with the cubs it is their mom, but officially the bears are genderless. Whether

patiently teaching the cubs to swim or lending a helping paw to push the Christmas tree home, Adult Bear sure appears to love those cubs.

It's an active family too. After celebrating with the cubs following a rousing game on the ice, look for the adult bear in family photos, then out playing a variety of sports with the cubs, and helping a cub put the star on the family Christmas tree.

Cubs—Are they twins? The original TV ad cast the two frisky cubs that way (and polar bears normally have between one and three cubs at a time). Always inquisitive. Always looking for fun. Always glad to share a Coke.

Seal—The Coca-Cola seal can now be seen frolicking with the cubs on many products. The seal, very popular as a bean bag toy, has become such a powerful spokesperson for Coca-Cola, its design also is a trademark.

Hollywood—When you see a bear in sunglasses leaning against a North Pole sign or vending machine, you've just caught "Hollywood" hard at work refreshing himself. You might even spy him with suitcase in hand on his way to Hollywood.

Attitude Bear—He's the hip-hop bear of the bunch. Crossed arms, jeans hanging down on his hips, and underwear showing (with a Coca-Cola band of course), this bear has attitude! When you're number one, what more can you say?

Sports Bear—What an athlete! He sails through the air on his skis with a smile on his face, turned to catch your attention. This sports enthusiast can be seen participating in all his favorite winter games, from snowboarding to skating.

What's Included

In *Coca-Cola Collectible Polar Bears*, we'll take an in-depth look at the hotter polar bear collectibles available, both in stores and on the secondary market. Many of the more collectible pieces contained in this book include price ranges. Other items, produced mostly for the mass market but deserving of inclusion nonetheless, are not priced.

When considering the potential value of a Coca-Cola polar bear piece, it is important to consider the condition of not only the item itself, but also of the packaging. Price ranges are for items and their packaging assumed to be in Near Mint to Mint condition. Most collectors look for Mint, unopened original boxes with all the original packaging intact.

But before we show you some of the more cherished Coca-Cola collectibles ever created, we'll provide some history of the bears that inspired them.

CHAPTER 1

The Coca-Cola Polar Bear Concept

"Polar Bear Swim," 1998

Polar bears holding chilled glasses of ice cold Coca-Cola were used in holiday advertisements as far back as 1926. But it wasn't until Edge Creative and Rhythm & Hues teamed up to produce the "Always Coca-Cola" campaign that polar bears became international favorites synonymous with the soft drink.

The television ad "Polar Bears" debuted in 1993, starring a group of sixteen bears who admire the Northern Lights while drinking ice-cold Coca-Cola. Though not a word is spoken, the striking computer-animated images catch the viewer's attention while the polar bears' light-hearted humor expresses the theme of good times with good friends.

Polar Bear 2000

Later in 1993, a second ad, "Holiday Polar Bear," celebrated the holiday season. Ice skating polar bears take a turn around a North Pole pond. When one takes a tumble while showing off his skating expertise, Santa helps him up. Together the two share holiday refreshment—a bottle of Coke, of course.

"Holiday Polar Bear (aka Skate)," 1993

In recognition of the Company's Olympic sponsorship of the 1994 Winter Games in Lillehammer, Norway, two more ads featured polar bears. "Olympic Polar Bear Ski Jump" and "Olympic Polar Bear Luge" depict these huggable bears enjoying their favorite Olympic sports with a bottle of Coke in hand.

"Olympic Polar Bear Ski Jump (aka Jump)," 1994

Polar Bear 2000

Twin polar bear cubs made their appearance in a holiday advertisement in 1994. "Holiday Polar Bear Twins" features two cubs struggling to push home a Christmas tree. An adult bear comes to the cubs' rescue in this humorous TV ad, and the family bonding tugs at the viewers' heartstrings.

A new friend is added to the ever-popular Arctic Circle in 1996 with the "Polar Bear/Baby Seal" commercial. When playful bear cubs lose their ball through a hole in the ice, a baby gray seal returns it with a flick of his nose. It seems only right that the cub expresses his thanks to his new friend by sharing a bottle of Coke. "Polar Bear Swim" produced in 1998 goes underwater to show the bear cubs learning to swim. One cub is rewarded with a Coke after "taking the plunge" into the arctic water.

"Polar Bear Swim," 1998

How the Polar Bears are Created

Created by the renowned ad agency Edge Creative, working with computer graphic specialists at Rhythm & Hues, the Coca-Cola polar bears have become one of the most recognized and beloved advertising images of all time.

These memorable advertisements undergo a lengthy production process, taking about twelve weeks from start to finish. A series of storyboards are designed, each representing one second of action. Pencil sketches illustrate the action on each board. Detail and background are then added.

To bring these Arctic characters to life, illustrators and animators study real polar bears and seals. How do they turn their heads? Move their bodies? Hold an object? Swim? Play? Relate to one another? Every movement is studied carefully before it is translated into animation.

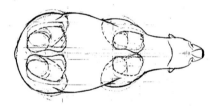

Polar bear concept drawings, Rhythm & Hues, 1992.

Polar Bear 2000

Scale models are constructed for each view of the polar bear to be used in the ad. Digital computer imaging and state-of-the-art graphics turn the schematic bear consisting of plotted points on a grid into three-dimensional images capable of walking, sitting and swimming.

Each change in position requires the bear's whole body to be re-plotted separately. Feet move while the torso leans forward. The neck turns as the mouth opens. Unlike living polar bears, each part of the computer-generated model is not connected, so each part must be moved independently.

Once basic movements are established, the bear is given detail. Fine motor movement enhances the image. Fur is added. Backgrounds are painted in. Lighting details are refined to give intricate reflections and shadows.

Finally music and sound are added. For the polar bears, that means a series of "oohs," "ahs" and grunts. Finished advertisements run just thirty seconds, but those brief moments have created strong bonds between collectors and these North Pole characters.

CHAPTER 2

Plush and Bean Bags

Who can resist the cuddly plush Coca-Cola polar bears? Whether you are a child wanting a hug from a plush friend or an adult in need of refreshing pause, these adorable plush bears can put a smile on your face.

Plush bears have been around for a while, but the world was introduced to a new icon when the Coca-Cola polar bears hit the market in 1993 to accompany their famous TV ads. The first stuffed polar bear with the familiar Coca-Cola red disc button on his chest was offered as a premium at a fast food chain. It made such a hit, a whole new collecting passion was born.

Hundreds of plush polar bears, in many sizes, outfits and designs, have followed. Most are made in China or Thailand from a furry soft plush fabric stuffed with polyester batting.

Some are quite talented, able to play music, move their arms or even ride a tricycle! They can be found just about anywhere from toy stores to grocery markets; through catalog sales and from chain retailers.

Communicorp, the first major manufacturer of Coca-Cola Polar Bear Plush, became Cavanagh Group International [CGI], the largest licensed manufacturer of Coca-Cola Polar Bear items. The Company's polar bears all have stitched smiles with shiny black eyes and molded plastic black noses. Soft and furry, they are the perfect size to hug. Their foot pads are sewn on black felt.

Many sizes have been made by CGI, from six-inch to forty-eight-inch versions. All carry the distinctive rectangular swing tag with the Always Bear on the front. Inside, the tag states: "You've seen him on TV delighting fans in millions of dens across the country. Now the lovable Coca-Cola Polar Bear is here with his polar buddies to warm the home of any family they join."

The Bear Everyone Is Thirsting After!
You've seen him on TV delighting fans in millions of dens across the country. Now the lovable **Coca-Cola** Polar Bear is

here with his polar buddies to warm the home of any family they join.

❄ ❄ ❄

Some come with a can of Coke, while others have a bottle of their favorite drink in hand. Many plush display Coca-Cola red disc buttons on their chests. One little guy even came in his own vinyl can of Coke. A few editions have dated feet. No matter what the size, what they are wearing or carrying, they are always cute and cuddly.

Another manufacturer of polar bear plush was Dakin, which began making Coca-Cola brand plush polar bears in 1994. Dakin polar bears come dressed in various apparel, from T-shirts to scarves, baseball caps to vests. The plush fur is not quite as long as the CGI editions and the bears' faces are more pointed.

Dakin Bears

Dakin bears are distinguished from CGI editions by their pointed faces and shorter fur.

Play-By-Play also produced some of the early Coca-Cola brand Polar Bears from 1994 to 1996. Early editions have long pointed noses and short coarse fur. Later polar bear faces grew softer and the plush fabric more snuggly. One very popular bear holds a red ball in his paws.

Cavanagh took over as the major manufacturer of Coca-Cola polar bears in 1996 and has produced dozens of lovable plush toys every year. Plush from CGI is manufactured specifically for several different markets. The company's "Mass" line is available at chain stores, primarily at Christmastime. The Heritage or "Gift" line is available year-round at gift stores,

Cavanagh produces the largest selection of plush polar bears in a variety of sizes.

Christmas shops and specialty retailers. Exclusive lines also are produced for specific stores such as Mediaplay (Musicland) and World of Coca-Cola in Atlanta.

In 1999, the Coca-Cola polar bear underwent a complete design change to make it more closely resemble the famous TV ads. Faces were made narrower with more complex stitching on the nose and mouth. Patches of gray fabric were sewn on the feet. Hands were stitched to resemble paws that grasped the larger bottles of Coke in a more realistic manner.

"New face" plush polar bears now are available with many different outfits, including a soda fountain jerk that can move its arms. The plush range in price from $25 to $50.

The centerpiece of many collections is a special 2000 polar bear in top hat and Coca-Cola scarf.

In 1999, Trendmasters issued a series of four Polar World Bears whose cheeks light up and who grunt when their paws are pushed. They all hold bottles of Coke and are clothed in different types of "arctic wear." The most unusual one wears a baseball cap backward and a plaid flannel shirt tied around its ample middle.

Topping other collector lists of Coca-Cola brand plush is the unique (and expensive) Steiff polar bear. Steiff, one of the finest makers of collectible plush bears in the world, created an heirloom Coca-Cola Polar Bear for its exclusive collection.

Limited to ten thousand, this bear is covered in mohair with jointed arms, airbrushed facial features, suede paws and knit scarf. The bear, holding a bottle of Coke, sports a red enamel Coca-Cola icon on his chest and a distinctive numbered tag in his ear. Surprisingly solid, this is not a floppy plush bear. The Steiff bear measures more than fifteen inches high from its seated position and is priced at $350 to $400.

FAO Schwarz offers the largest polar bear around that is not only enormous at four feet tall, but also the most huggable edition ever made. This giant bear is made of the softest plush with trademark Coca-Cola "new face" eyes and sculpted black nose. With stitched paws and feet, children can literally lose themselves in the arms of this polar bear classic.

Coke and the Bean Bag Craze

Combining the most recognized trademark with the hottest new collecting passion, Coca-Cola brand bean bag plush took the world by storm in 1997.

Cavanagh produced different lines of bean bag plush that sent polar bear collectors scurrying to stores. One line is the Mass (or mass market) line. Like the plush, these bean bags are sold at chain stores primarily at Christmastime.

Released with the seasons and consisting of a set of six cuddly characters, each set has at least three polar bears along with various other Arctic friends (including a penguin, seal, walrus, husky

and even a Coke can). Sets retire each year and have a distinctive swing tag that is numbered, titled and dated.

Retailers may sell bean bags as sets of six or individually (convenient for collectors of polar bears exclusively), and each decides which line to carry and how many cases to order.

To date, there have been eight sets of mass bean bags. They retail for $36–42 a set and rapidly rise in value when retired. The original Spring 1997 Mass set now retails for $60–90 a set. Here's a sampling of each Mass line set:

Spring 1997 Mass Set

The first set of six, still available on the secondary market.

Winter 1997 Mass Set

These bean bags found their way into convenience stores, drug stores, and gas stations.

Spring 1998 Mass Set

The #0131 Polar Bear in Argyle Shirt was a huge hit as new outfits were introduced.

Winter 1998 Mass Set

The two polar bears in this set are hardest to find.

Everyday 1999 Set

Production problems caused delays and a temporary hike in prices on the secondary market.

Winter 1999 Set

Polar Bear in Long Striped Cap was the first to disappear from store shelves.

Year 2000 Set

In addition to special 2000 apparel, these bean bags came with special double tags, stating "Exclusive 2000 design."

Everyday 2000 Set

One polar bear in this summer release sports a delivery outfit and cap; the other a soda jerk outfit.

Another line of hot bean bag plush produced by CGI is the Heritage gift line available at fine gift stores, Christmas shops and specialty outlets year-round. These sets are produced in single runs, so they are more limited in number and availability. Like the Mass line, they come out in sets of six, usually twice a year.

Many of the Heritage sets are themed, such as the 2000 Career set where each of the characters wears the uniform of a different occupation. Here is a sampling of each set:

Spring Heritage Set 1998

A reindeer, walrus and can of Coke with sunglasses debuted in this set, but the two polar bears remained collector favorites.

Winter Heritage Set 1998

Three polar bears highlight this set of six bean bags, featuring very detailed outfits.

POG and GCC Exclusives 1998

Two groups of retailers, Gift Creation Concepts (GCC) and Parade of Gift Retailers (POG) joined forces with Cavanagh in 1998 to distribute two exclusive Coca-Cola polar bears with exclusive accessories.

GCC Exclusive 1999

The "new face" Polar Bear in Red Romper was well received by some and hated by others. Regardless, this bear sold well.

New retailers joined the Coca-Cola bean bag bandwagon with this set, which featured four polar bears and two seals in sports attire. Bears released actually sported "new" faces, unlike the "old face" bears in this rare prototype set.

Career Set 2000

Every detail was accounted for in the production of this set, showcasing a polar bear fireman, construction worker and policeman.

Cavanagh also offers exclusive bean bags for a particular chain of stores, restaurants, or for a particular event. These generally are the most collectible bean bags of all and are grabbed up immediately by collectors.

Other manufacturers produce Coca-Cola brand bean bag plush for an international market that continues to grow each year. Special editions have been released in England, Germany, Australia, New Zealand and Hong Kong to the delight of collectors around the world.

Musicland/Media Play Exclusive 1997

A scarce polar bear that sold for $5.99 at Musicland and Media Play stores during the 1997 Christmas season. Some stores first required a $25 purchase.

For more detailed information and pricing on Coca-Cola bean bags and plush toys, pick up a copy of another book in the Coca-Cola Collector Series, *Coca-Cola Collectible Bean Bags and Plush.*

Manchu Wok Bear 1998

Diners at Manchu Wok in the U.S. and Canada who purchased a
combo meal with a large Coca-Cola were allowed to buy the bear
for the suggested retail price of $2.99.

CHAPTER 3

Polar Bear Christmas

Christmas is the best time for Coca-Cola polar bears. Just about everything you can think of to decorate your home for the holidays—snowglobes, stocking holders, bells, table toppers, tree skirts, Christmas lights and hundreds of ornaments—feature the antics of the fun-loving polar bears.

Ornaments

Ornaments comprise one of the larger areas of collectible polar bear products available.

Kurt Adler, known for European style glass ornaments, has produced several Polonaise polar bear ornaments. (Polonaise refers to a special reflective finish fused onto the glass.) From small cubs in a stocking to bear faces on glass balls to large smiling bears, each Adler piece is intricately crafted.

Cavanagh Group International (CGI) is one of the larger producers of polar bear items. This Atlanta-area company offers several lines of collector polar bear ornaments each year. Chrome finish

bottle cap ornaments from 1997–1999 pictured various polar bear scenes, and polar bears also have sat atop several of CGI's contour bottle ornaments. Mid-size and mini-ornaments abound with polar bears. Mercury glass bear figurines were released in 1998 and 1999.

In recognition of the popularity of the Coca-Cola polar bears, CGI started the Polar Bear ornament line in 1994. For avid Christmas polar bear collectors, here is a list of ornament line issues to date:

Polar Bear Ornament Line

Title	Description	Item#	Issued	Retired
Down Hill Sledder	Polar bear lying on a sled	12101	1994	1996
North Pole Delivery	Polar bear in snowshoes with sack of Coke	12102	1994	1995
Skating Coca-Cola Polar Bear	Polar bear on ice skates	12103	1994	1995
Vending Machine Mischief	Polar bear sneaking a Coke	12104	1994	1996
Polar Bear on Bottle Opener	Polar bear sitting on bottle opener	12105	1995	1997
Snowboardin' Bear	Polar bear on snowboard	12106	1995	1997
The Christmas Star	Polar bear holding cub putting star on tree	12108	1996	1998
Hollywood	Polar bear rest at North Pole sign	12109	1996	1999
Downhill Racers	Polar bear adult and cub	CA0205	1997	
Double the Fun	Two cubs at vending machine	CA0206	1997	1998
	Polar bear on fountain machine	CA0207	1998	
	Polar bear with Coke sled	CA0208	1998	
	Polar bear and cub with gifts	CA0209	1999	
	Polar bear on juke box	CA0210	1999	
	Polar bear with Year 2000 top hat	CA0211	1999	

Cavanagh added the Bear Cub ornament line in 1997. The line depicts the playful cubs and their friends playing in many humorous poses, always with their favorite drink right at their fingertips.

Bear Cub Ornament Line

Title	Description	Item	Issued	Retired
Baby's First Christmas	Baby sleeping on six-pack	CA0601	1997	1998
Cookies for Santa	Cub making Christmas cookies	CA0602	1997	1998
Dreaming of a Magical Christmas	Cub napping on rocking chair	CA0603	1997	1997
A Refreshing Ice Cold Treat	Cub sitting on ice cube	CA0604	1997	
Twas the Night before Christmas	Cub reading book	CA0605	1997	
Stocking Stuffer Surprise	Cub sitting on top of stocking	CA0606	1997	1997
	Seal on ball	CA0607	1998	
	Seal on ice cube	CA0608	1998	
	Cub and penguin on sled	CA0609	1999	
	Cub with wreath	CA0610	1999	

Prices range from $7–8 for current editions to $20–25 for retired ones. For current editions, check retail chains, Christmas shops, gift stores, Hallmark stores and outlet stores during the holidays for these special ornaments. Some secondary market sources still have retired editions available. Internet stores and auctions also carry these Christmas favorites.

One of the most popular lines of ornaments made by CGI is the polar bear plush ornaments. The Cuppa Bear Series (plush bear inside a mug) was produced only in 1997.

Twenty-four different editions of plush ornaments have been released since 1995. Usually six new editions come out each year featuring polar bears and their Arctic friends: the penguin, walrus, reindeer and seal.

They retail for $5–6 each or $30 for a set of six and are available during the holidays from a wide variety of stores.

Plush Ornament Line (polar bears only)

Description	Item#	Issued	Retired
Polar bear with red earmuffs	19101	1995	1997
Polar bear with bowtie	19102	1995	1997
Polar bear with red Santa hat	19103	1995	1997
Polar bear with package and Coke	19104	1995	1997
Stand-up polar bear with red earmuffs	19105	1996	1997
Stand-up polar bear with bowtie	19106	1996	1997
Stand-up polar bear with red Santa hat	19107	1996	1997
Stand-up polar bear with package	19108	1996	1997
Polar bear with stocking and Coke	CA0501	1997	1997
Stand-up polar bear with red vest	CA0502	1997	1997
Polar bear with skates	CA0503	1997	1998
Polar bear with red tee shirt	CA0504	1997	1997
Stand-up polar bear in stocking	CA0505	1997	1998
Bear with hat and star	CA0515	1999	
Polar bear with red bow and gift	CA0518	1999	

Cuppa Bear Line

Description	Item#	Issued	Retired
Always friends mug with polar bear with package ornament	92007	1996	1997
Always fun mug with polar bear in red ear muffs ornament	92008	1996	1997
Coke stand mug with polar bear in red Santa hat ornament	92009	1996	1997
Service with a smile mug with polar bear with bowtie ornament	92010	1996	1997

Cavanagh released a collection of Trim.A.Tree ornaments for a major chain store during a three-year period. The ornaments all lay flat, and the boxes are marked "Available Exclusively at TARGET."

Elves and polar bears coexist in the Mid-Size ornament collection by Cavanagh. Most of the ornaments in this popular and creative series, featuring planes, parachutes and unicycles, were released and retired the same year.

Mid-Size Ornament Collection

Title	Description	Item#	Issued	Retired
All Aboard the North Pole Express	Polar bear on train	17101	1996	1997
Look Out Below	Elf and parachute	17103	1996	1997
North Pole Express	Elf in airplane	17104	1996	1997
For You	Elf with six pack	17107	1996	1997
	Elf on reindeer	17102	1996	1996
	Puppy holding six pack	17106	1996	1996
Ski Jump	Polar bear with skis	17109	1996	1996
	Elf in car	17105	1996	1996
Stocking Stuffer	Polar bear in stocking	17110	1996	1996
	Elf on sled	17108	1996	1996

Title	Description	Item#	Issued	Retired
	Polar bear on snowshoes with cub	17112	1996	1996
	Polar bear on unicycle	17111	1996	1996
Friends Forever	Polar bear and penguin in bottle cap	CA0705	1997	1997
Christmas Dreamer	Penguin on moon	CA0606	1997	1997
Cool Capers	Polar bear and vending machine	CA0607	1997	1997
Downhill Sledders	Polar bears on sled	CA0708	1997	1997

Cavanagh Mid-Size Ornament Collection

Cavanagh Mid-Size Ornament Collection

O ther random polar bear ornaments abound. Be on the lookout for blue round balls with various polar bear scenes from Enesco; sets of polar bears enjoying their favorite winter sports; cubs decked out for winter fun; and flat metal stars with a polar bear cameo in the center.

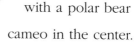

Miscellaneous Polar Bear Ornaments

Stocking Holders

Cavanagh manufactures Coca-Cola brand stocking holders, many of which feature polar bears. Made from a metal composite cast, each holder is heavy enough to perch on a mantle, window ledge or table-top with ease. They retail for $18–25. Here is a sampling:

Year	Description	Item#
1995	Coca-Cola Polar Bear (waving)	45003
1997	Cool Tidings Bear (at vending machine)	CE0201
	Trimming the Tree Bears (decorating tree)	CE0202
	Waiting for Santa Cubs (at the fireplace)	CE0203
	All the Trimmings Cub (decorating tree)	CE0204
1998	Refreshing Fun Polar Bear (with cub and seal)	CE2101
	Cool Refreshment Polar Bear (and six pack)	CE0205
	Just for You Polar Bear (and cubs with presents)	CE0206

Other Christmas Items

Our winter friends also can be found on such varied holiday items as:

• **Table toppers**: Large figurines made of fused glass that may work as table centerpieces or decorating items.

• **Tree skirts**: Add charm to your Christmas tree with a quilted tree skirt emblazoned with polar bears.

• **Bells:** Ring in the holidays with bells decorated with polar bears. A polar bear sits atop a glass bell with an ice cube hanging in the center in one unique edition.

- **Holiday Popcorn Tins**: Great for gift giving and snacking, tins come in all sizes and shapes and are decorated with favorite polar bear scenes.

- **Snowglobes:** Dozens of wintry scenes in glass balls capture the polar bear fantasy. Some play music. Others dance with movement. All delight the young and young-at-heart. We'll examine these in detail in a later chapter.

- **Wrapping paper, cards, gift tags:** Everything a polar bear lover could need for gift giving.

What more could you ask? How about Christmas cards by the dozens.

CHAPTER 4

Polar Bears
from A to Z

T he ever-popular Coca-Cola Polar Bears appear on all kinds of products, giving collectors plenty of options when building their collections. Although several manufacturers may offer a particular trademark item for sale, each design is uniquely licensed by The Coca-Cola Company. We've listed manufacturers, possible sources and suggested prices. In Chapter 5, we list resources for polar bear products. Ask your local store employees if they carry these product lines or if they will order for you directly from the manufacturers. Keep your eyes open at swap meets, collector gatherings and on the Internet.

Animation Cels

Taken from actual imagery seen in the original TV polar bear commercials, Name That Toon of California produces hand-painted animation cels. Each digital scene is first printed onto celluloid acetate. More than 120 hours goes into creating fine resolution artwork on which every detail is brilliantly painted and digitally enhanced to produce an

exact recreation of the commercial image. The average production run is two thousand pieces.

Cels are named and come with a certificate of authenticity. They cost between $100 and $400 apiece. Lithograph prints made from these cels cost between $25 and $50 each. Animation cells are available at fine gift stores and collectible retailers as well as a few Internet stores.

Backpacks

Two editions of children's backpacks can be found in specialty shops, toy stores and on the Internet for $18–30. The first edition, Aviator Bear, is a plush polar bear dressed in a flight jacket with cap and goggles. The second edition, Polar Bear Family, distributed by Jaygur Imports of Canada, is the Attitude Bear in jean pants holding a baby polar bear.

Balls

Coca-Cola polar bears have appeared on every conceivable kind of ball: basket-balls, footballs, volleyballs, soccer balls, beach balls and bowling balls. One toy ball featuring an outline drawing of a polar bear from Buztronics, Inc. even flashes with red lights when bounced.

Banks

Polar bear banks come in many shapes and sizes. From Ertl Collectibles comes the 1/43 scale Coca-Cola Stearman Bi-Plane (with polar bear and cub) bank. Ertl also makes a polar bear mechanical bank featur-ing the famous TV star gazing into the sky as he grins and guzzles a bottle of Coke on an ice

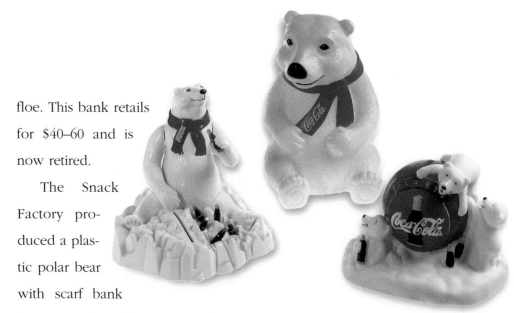

floe. This bank retails for $40–60 and is now retired.

The Snack Factory produced a plastic polar bear with scarf bank that is now retired. From Canada comes another plastic polar bear bank with two cubs frolicking with a large red ball while a third cub relaxes in the snow drinking a Coke. Enesco offers earthenware with a polar bear delivery man on an ice floe to hold your change and a snow surfing bear holding a Coke bank.

Barbie

Mattel has made thousands of "Barbie" dolls, but only one comes with a Coca-Cola polar bear.

"Party Barbie" is holding a mini-polar bear in her hand along with a bottle of Coke. The box, with polar bears on the walls, opens into a play scene. Retired in 1999, it retails for $25–40.

Blankets, Throws, Pillows, Towels

In an exclusive Wal-Mart design, polar bears holding bottles of Coke in their paws decorate a blanket. Other designs available at retail chains and gift stores depict polar bear faces, polar bears drinking Coke or cubs and seals at play. Images appear on various styles of blankets, throws, pillows and towels. Look anywhere bedding and linen are sold and expect to pay $20–40 each.

Bottles

For all the millions of bottles The Coca-Cola Company has produced, just a handful have pictured polar bears. These special edition bottles are some of the most valuable ever issued.

In 1994, Hot August Nights, an annual vintage car race in Reno, Nevada, issued a commemorative three-bottle set in a gift box that featured a 1950s polar bear complete with guitar and Reno sign. (The bottles issued for the set have vintage cars on them, not polar bears.) This boxed edition is valued at $50–60.

A very rare bottle issued in 1994 carries a picture of a partying polar bear wishing everyone a "Merry Christmas from College Park and Marietta Production." This bottle is valued at $250 today.

A similarly-styled polar bear appears on a special bottle from the South Metro bottling division in Atlanta in 1994 with "Happy Holidays 1994 South Metro" on the label. It is valued at $200.

The Coca-Cola Collectors Club issued a bottle with the Always Polar Bear for its Smokeyfest convention held in Gatlinburg, Tennessee, May 19–21, 1994. This bottle sells for $40–45.

The Tulsa Zoo's newly remodeled polar bear exhibit issued a special fund-raising bottle in 1994. The bottle for the Polar Care "Build the Bear Necessities" campaign depicts a child's drawing of a polar bear face and is valued at $8–15.

The Coca-Cola Collectors Club issued a pair of bottles for its 1995 Ohio Winterfest convention held in Zanesville, Ohio. One pictures a smiling polar bear holding a bottle of Coke and the other pictures Santa handing a bottle of Coke. The two bottle set in gift box is valued at $250–300. This pair of bottles is highly prized as the last small-order bottles authorized by The Coca-Cola Company.

The Coca-Cola Collectors Club Convention in 1996 held in Reston, Virginia issued a special polar bear with American flag bottle. The artwork, unique to the convention, was also used on a Winross toy tanker truck, T-shirt and deck of cards produced for the event and available only to attendees. The bottle is valued at $35–40.

In 1996 Sunbelt Marketing offered a limited edition gold bottle with the skiing polar bear. Gold bottles are made from real glass contour bottles electroplated with a gold film. Now very hard to find, it sells for $25–35.

The 2000 gathering of the annual McDonald's Owner/Operators Convention held in Orlando, Florida produced one of the most unique and rare polar bear bottles to date: "Being the Best! Around the Corner, Around the World. Orlando, 2000."

Made by Sunbelt Marketing especially for this convention, the eight-inch, hinged contour bottle is painted dark brown and green with a red cap. On the outside, the polar bear sits on one side and Ronald McDonald sits on the other. When the resin bottle is opened, a section of globe appears on the left with the Golden Arches sign sprouting against a background of the heavens. Ronald McDonald and the polar bear pilot a rocket soaring across the right toward a McDonald's sign on the moon.

Cameras

In the 1970s, the Coca-Cola trademark was first seen on a Polaroid camera. Several editions from Japan followed over the years shaped like Coke cans. In the 1990s the market was flooded with disposable cameras, several with the Coca-Cola name. Ansco produced the Coke Year 2000 Collector Camera in 1999 that comes in a tin box decorated for Christmas.

Clocks

Several manufacturers have featured the smiling polar bears on their clocks. Attitude Bear and Always Bear clocks sell at retail chain stores, craft stores and gift shops for $20–25.

Wake up with a lounging polar bear wearing sunglasses and holding a bottle of Coke in each hand. This whimsical digital alarm clock plays the "Always Coca-Cola" jingle.

Cavanagh recently released a musical clock shaped like a bottle of Coke that opens up to reveal a smiling polar bear. Standing eighteen inches tall and retailing for $30, this clock no doubt will appear in thousands of homes soon.

General Time Corporation (Westclox in Canada) offers several polar bear clocks available in higher-end retail and gift stores for $25–50 each. One small green clock features the polar bear enjoying a Coke while a small bottle swings on the pendulum.

Clothing

Many manufacturers have produced all kinds of sports and leisure wear with the Coca-Cola label. Baseball caps, tee shirts, sweatshirts, ties, jackets, sweaters have sported polar bears. Popular tee shirt styles show the polar bears competing in various sports, advertising special events and relaxing with their favorite drink.

Collector Plates

The world–famous Franklin Mint has produced a steady supply of Coca-Cola polar bear collector plates. These limited edition hand-painted and hand-numbered plates are very collectible. They originally sell for $40–50, but quickly rise to $100–150 once retired.

Retired editions include a three-plate series begun in 1995. All feature a bright light blue aura and silver rims that leave the polar bears aglow. The first 8-1/2 inch plate depicts a single adult bear with a bottle of Coke. In 1996, a second plate took a scene from the TV ad depicting three bears skating on a pond. The third plate in the series, also released in 1996, was taken from the first TV ad showing a community of bears watching the Northern Lights in the sky.

A ten-inch white plate from the Franklin Mint displaying the message, "Seasons Greetings 1994" also features a Coca-Cola polar bear.

A smiling Coca-Cola polar bear surrounded by a holly wreath decorated with Coca-Cola ornaments wishes you the best. A large red bow with "Always" appears at the bottom of this retired collector's plate.

Computer Accessories

Now you can mouse around your computer on a Coca-Cola polar bear mousepad.

Computer Expressions manufactured the pads, which usually retail for $10–15 each. Five editions, carrying the following polar bear images, have been released to date: 1995 polar bear with bottle; 1996, bear wearing a Coca-Cola baseball cap with baseball and bat; 1996, bear hanging on a basketball rim; 1996, Coca-Cola rocket ship carrying adult bear and cubs to the heavens where one constellation of stars resembles a contour bottle; 1996, three bears mountain climbing up a contour bottle made of ice (the rarest of the group).

The Coca-Cola Company website offers a free polar bear screen saver featuring ski-jumping bears flying across your computer screen. Visit www.coca-cola.com.

Cookie Jars

Cookie jars featuring polar bears are very collectible. Cavanagh has produced an annual collector edition polar bear cookie jar since 1995 for its Heritage (Gift) line. Originally retailing for $28–35, the jars have rapidly increased in price when retired to $100–150 for the harder-to-find first editions. Here's a list to help you identify each one:

Cavanagh Heritage Line Cookie Jars

Year	Description	Item#
1995	Polar bear in green sweater and hat	H91005
1996	Hollywood sitting with suitcase	H76005
1997	Hollywood leaning against vending machine	H76008
1998	Polar bear leaning against six pack	HN0604
1999	Polar bear in red delivery truck	HJ1702
1999	Media Play Exclusive polar bear in green delivery truck	HJ1703
2000	Panda	HJ1704
2000	Bears at jukebox	HJ1705

CGI also makes collectible cookie jars for the Mass retail line:

Cavanagh Mass Line Cookie Jars

Year	Description	Item#
1994	Always Cool Bear	91051
1996	Christmas polar bear cookie jar (Santa hat)	91056
1998	Polar bear with large bottle	CJ0202
1998	Three bears at vending machine	CJ0203
1999	Bear at soda fountain	CJ1401

Sunbelt Marketing makes an unusual white ceramic cookie jar with interchangeable collector lids. One lid depicts polar bear cubs at play. Cookie jars with lids range from $75–85 retail.

Die-Cast Cars

The NASCAR Thunder Special Motegi Coca-Cola 500, held in Motegi City, Japan on November 22, 1998, is the inspiration behind a number of top collectibles featuring Dale Earnhardt Jr. and the Coke polar bear car logo. Limited edition

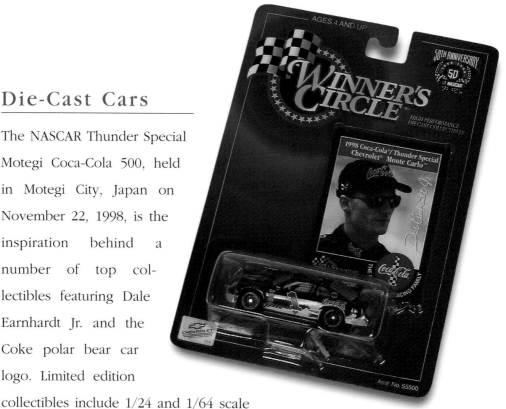

collectibles include 1/24 and 1/64 scale replicas of the Coke polar bear car, 1/4 scale polar bear racing helmets, and even a gas pump, all from Action Performance Corporation. Suggested prices range from $14–20 for 1/64 scale to $80–85 for 1/24 scale cars. Helmets retail for $40–45 each.

The most incredible collector piece commemorating this race is a solid lead crystal replica of the polar bear car in 1/24 scale. An intricately etched polar bear on the hood makes this piece an outstanding collectible. Retail prices for this limited edition treasure range between $160–200. Other die-cast cars featuring the Coca-Cola Polar Bear have been made by Revell and Winners Circle. Hasbro produced a pit-row scene and several die-cast model cars.

Dishes, Bowls, Platters

Enesco Corporation produced a line of polar bear dishes in 1998 that included platters, serving bowls, canisters, cups, mugs, napkin holder, sugar and creamer, spoon rest, and teapot all with a distinctive polar bear drinking a bottle of Coke. Items retail for $15–$100.

Zak Designs distributed a hard-to-find set of children's dishes with polar bears in 1995. Kids are entertained by the affectionate adult bear and laughing cubs while eating with the plates, bowls and glasses.

Figurines

Many companies have produced Coca-Cola polar bear figurines. Three manufacturers stand out as having produced the most collectible lines:

• Franklin Mint—This collectibles company has produced several sculptured figurine polar bears in its Coca-Cola collectors series. Polar bears fishing, cubs playing, cubs playing with a seal and polar bears trimming the Christmas tree are scenes featured in Franklin Mint's porcelain collector box series that retails for $30–40 each.

• Enesco Corporation—manufactured several collectible lines of earthenware polar bear figurines that retire every couple of years. The individual figurines have a suggested retail price of $15–17.50 each. Sets include: the 1999 International Polar Bears, 1998 Professional Bears, Coke Bear Home Holiday, Always Love, Always Coca-Cola Valentine series, and 1997 Snow Sports.

• Cavanagh—Has featured collector polar bear figurines in its Heritage (Gift Store) line since 1994. Polar bear and polar bear cub figurines are very popular. Here is a list of figurines to look for:

Cavanagh Heritage Figurines

Name	Description	Item #	Issue	Retired
Coca-Cola Polar Bear and Friend	2 polar bears on an ice base	H23004	1994	1998
Coca-Cola Polar Bear and Friends	8 polar bears on wood base	H23003	1994	1998
Always	Polar bear family	H23010	1995	1996
Coca-Cola Stand	Cubs selling Coke with adult bear	H77002	1996	1998
Decorating the Tree	Bear lifting cub to put star on tree	H77003	1996	1996
Playing with Dad	Bear playing with cubs	H77004	1996	1996
Cool Break	Hollywood on chaise lounge	H77005	1996	1998
Refreshing Treat	Bear and cubs at vending machine	H77007	1996	1996
Gone Fishing	Bear and cub ice fishing	H77008	1996	1997
Downhill Derby	Bear and cubs on sled	H77006	1997	1998
Mama Look! Is He a Bear Too?	Polar bears with seal	H77010	1997	1998
Times with Dad are Special	Bear and cub at vending machine	H77011	1997	1998
On the Road to Adventure	Polar Bear at billboard	H77012	1997	1998
On the Road to Adventure	Bear and seal at cooler	HN0201	1998	
Friends Make the Job Easier	Bear, cub, seal with vending mach.	HN0202	1998	
Rub a Dub Dub	Bears bathing a seal	HN0203	1998	1998
C is for Coca-Cola	Adult bear reading to cubs	HN0204	1998	1998
The Perfect Refreshment	Polar bear, cub, penguin with cart	HN0205	1999	
A Special Treat	Polar bear and cub at soda fountain	HN0206	1999	

In addition, Cavanagh has made more than sixty different figurines in its Polar Bear Cubs collection since 1996.

Some of the most collectible polar bear figurines are offered through the Cavanagh Coca-Cola Collectors Society. Members of the society receive free sign-up gifts, personalized cards and certificates, quarterly newsletters, members-only special offers, the annual Product and Retail Information Catalog and advance information on upcoming events and products. Members-only polar bear figurines include:

Cavanagh Coca-Cola Collectors Society Figurines

Year	Title	How attained
1996	Hollywood	Sign-up gift
1997	Always Friends	Sign-up gift
1998	Passing the Day in a Special Way	Sign-up gift
1998	I Belong	Special purchase
1999	Hearing from You is a Special Treat	Sign-up gift
2000	Family Time is a Special Treat	Sign-up gift

Glasses, Mugs

Indiana Glass is the largest manufacturer of Coca-Cola brand glassware. Polar bear editions include the Attitude Bear, Always Bear, Cubs and Seal. Indiana Glass also produces a thirteen-inch glass platter with the Always Bear. Many retail, chain and department stores carry Indiana Glass products in bulk or boxed sets. Individual glasses retail for $2–6 apiece. Platters sell for $25–28 each.

Hundreds of polar bear mugs have been made. Gift Creations has several Coca-Cola polar bears in its line of mugs, retailing for $5–7 each.

Cavanagh produced many coffee (soup, hot chocolate, etc.) mugs with various polar bear scenes. Mugs are becoming more collectible because editions are retired each year. Prices vary between $7–15 each. Here's a breakdown of CGI mugs:

Cavanagh Mugs

Year	Description	Item#
1996	"Always Friends Cub" offers polar bear a Coke	92001
	"Always Fun" polar bear and cubs sitting on stomach	92002
	"Coke Stand" bear drinking at a cub Coke stand	92003
	"Service with a Smile" penguin serving bear on chaise lounge	92004
	"Always Refreshing" polar bear looking at Coke bottle	92005
	"Push Me, Pull Me" polar bear playing with cubs	92006
1997	Ice skating bear	CL0201
	"To Grandmother's house we go" cub with sled	CL0203
	"Clubhouse" bear cub club	CL0205
1998	Half circle design	CL0207
	Postcards	CL0208
	Winter sports	CL0209
	Rollerblading polar bear	CL0210
	Skiing Polar Bear	CL0211
	Hollywood with Coca-Cola	CL0212

Greeting Cards

Polar bear greeting cards, available especially around Valentines Day and Christmastime, delight by depicting scenes from the famous TV ads. The quality ranges from slick, inexpensive print to finely detailed linen-type paper.

For Valentines Day 2000, Mello Smello offered sticker valentines with eight different polar bear cards and stickers. They were available at grocery stores for less than ten cents a card.

Classico of California has just produced a new line of Coca-Cola postcards, several of which feature favorite polar bear scenes.

Jewelry

Likenesses of our furry friends have graced pins, necklaces and earrings in all kinds, shapes and sizes.

Cavanagh sold plush to a watch manufacturer, which produced two Coca-Cola watches. One edition comes packaged with a mini-collectible bean bag bear, while the other comes with a larger collectible plush bear. The two styles of watches feature the

face of a bear and a bear relaxing. They were a big hit at large chain stores during Christmas of 1999, then quickly disappeared. Collectors must search the secondary market to find them. Expect to pay $20–25.

Key Chains

Several manufacturers produce Coca-Cola key chains with polar bear images. Buckles of America makes several pewter polar bear key chains retailing for $7–10 each. Plastic key chains abound with Coca-Cola Polar Bear images ranging in price from $2–$8. Gift Creations has several metal key chains with polar bear images priced between $5–8. They are larger editions of their famous line of polar bear pins.

General Time Corporation manufactures a snowboarding bear keychain with LCD display that also comes with a matching magnet. Aminco offers several styles of key chains with the Coca-Cola polar bear.

Kitchen Accessories

Where do you begin to list the thousands of items produced with the Coca-Cola polar bear? Here are some examples of products available for your home:

Gift Creations offered a six-inch ceramic tile trivet for $6, as well as collector spoons featuring a polar bear for $5–6 each.

Shadle Enterprises, known for its giftware and houseware line featuring Coca-Cola, makes a wastebasket with a polar bear family that retails for $15.

Several manufacturers offer aprons, ceramic teapots, dishes, coasters, napkin holders, steins, serving trays—anything you could imagine with a polar bear motif.

Lamps, Nightlights, Light Switch Covers

Light your home with a Coca-Cola Polar Bear lamp. A smiling bear lampshade sits atop a large bottle cap base.

Leave a bear in charge of lighting up your nights with a Coca-Cola Polar Bear nightlight.

One edition shows the Attitude Bear with a denim shade.

Decorate your kitchen, bathroom, bedroom or office with a

polar bear light switch cover. Produced in 1994, this rare retired plastic cover comes in the form of a full-length polar bear.

Lunchboxes

What child wouldn't like to take his or her lunch to school in a polar bear lunchbox? Scenes of happy cubs highlight this group made by Aladdin in 1996. Lunchboxes come with a thermal beverage holder and are now retired.

Magnets

Coca-Cola magnets remain plentiful in all shapes and sizes. Polar
bear magnets by Aminco are
reminiscent of the famous
advertising, including a happy
bear lifting his bottle of Coke, a
bear looking at a bottle and a
bear ski jumping. Other editions feature a
polar bear in ski goggles, a bear family
drinking Coke and a Fourth of July Bear.
These magnets retail between $3–4
apiece.

   Some of the most popular Arjon magnets are the small plush polar bears in red scarves
with magnets in the paws. So far, there

are just two styles of polar bears and one seal. You can find them in markets, chain stores and drug stores for $5–6.

Buckles of America makes a pewter polar bear skiing magnet that retails for $7–8 each.

Other editions have been produced by many different manufacturers and can be found in markets, toy stores and stationers.

Milk Caps

Not to be left out of any collectible craze, the Coca-Cola Polar Bears found their faces on milk caps. These small cardboard circles became a collecting goal for kids and adults in the early 1990s.

Musicals

Enesco action musicals feature earthenware polar bears that play such favorite tunes as "Always Coca-Cola," "I'd Like to Buy the World a Coke" and "It's the Real Thing." One edition features a bear trimming his tree. Another edition features the bear with a sack of Coke bottles by the fireplace. Other musicals (such as the Cavanagh edition pictured on the next page) depict bears sledding, fishing and delivering a case of Coke. A soda shop is the scene for still another musical figure. Musicals retail for $30–40. Editions retire every year.

The Franklin Mint created a happy animated musical Coca-Cola truck filled with polar bears all enjoying winter recreation. A seal watches the cubs from on top of the truck. Musicals retail for $200–225.

By far the largest collection of musical polar bears comes from CGI—snow globe musicals, mini-musicals, ceramic musicals and multi-movement musicals, all available at large chain stores, department stores and retailers. From the Heritage Collection comes several exclusive musicals featuring

animated polar bears and cubs dancing, singing and moving to famous
Coke jingles found at gift and collectible stores. Musicals retail from
$30 to $80, depending on complexity of design and movement.

Photo Frames

Cavanagh produces the largest
assortment of photo frames featuring polar bears. Enesco also
produces polar bear frames.
You can display your photo
surrounded by polar bears in
various poses for $15–40.

Speaking of photos,
everyone loves the giant
polar bear in the lobby of
the World of Coca-Cola store
in Atlanta or Las Vegas. Sit
on his lap for a photo, but
watch out for a surprise.

Pins and Pin Sets

Collectors love polar bear pins. Good sources for Coca-Cola pins include World of Coca-Cola stores, and pin collector websites everywhere.

Aminco offers several styles of pins, magnets, key chains and luggage tags all featuring the smiling Coca-Cola polar bear. The Polar Bear Fun series pictures cubs enjoying all kinds of winter activities. The fourteen-pin set retails for $7.

Gift Creations offers many hand-painted, enamel-on-brass collectible pins, jumbo pins and sets of polar bear pins. The winter sports bear sets are especially delightful. Skiing, skating, snowboarding, ski jumping and snowmobiling polar bears always have a smile and a bottle of Coke. These happy bear images also adorn key chains, bottle openers, earrings and thimbles.

Framed pin sets are wonderful items to collect. Limited production, special editions and wood-framed displays help to make pin sets quite collectible and valuable. In 1997, a limited edition of twenty-five hundred pins pictures a train depot in the mountains with an adult bear and cubs on a billboard up on the roof. Six pins shaped like train cars sit on the tracks. Originally costing $100, this set now sells for $150 or more. Another framed edition features four jumbo polar bear sports pins.

Playing Cards/Trading Cards

Every Christmas, Bicycle Company and United States Playing Card Company produce Coca-Cola brand playing cards with various holiday and nostalgic scenes. These cards and mini-cards have depicted polar bears for several years. Some even come with a clip that snaps the deck to your pants. Card prices vary with the year, but they usually retail for less than $20.

Some examples include:

Year	Description	Size
1997	Attitude Bear in front of a red and yellow sunburst	single deck
1998	Polar bear cooling off in a Coke machine with soccer ball	double deck
1998	Mountain climbing polar bear reaching for Coke	double deck
1999	Sports bears skateboarding	mini-deck

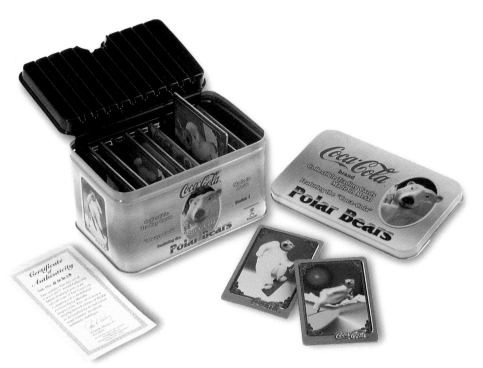

Metal collector's cards in a tin box became very popular in the Nineties. The Coca-Cola Company produced several editions featuring famous advertising artwork, slogans and memorabilia. The metal cards are embossed with artwork on the front and have history and information on the back. Polar bear collectors cherish the set that features polar bear art. Many of the scenes are from the famous TV ads, but there are also cards with new art versions of the animals at play.

A limited edition game of Uno featured polar bears in a collector's tin in 1998. The game retailed for $25.

Porcelain Boxes

Midwest of Cannon Falls brings us tiny treasures of miniature artwork in hand-painted porcelain boxes. The Coca-Cola polar bear edition is quite unusual as the bear is flocked with simulated fur. A tiny bottle of Coke rests inside the hinged box. Porcelain boxes have served as treasured keepsakes for hundreds of years.

Puzzles

Jigsaw puzzles, puzzles in tins, mini-puzzles and canister puzzles offer various challenging Coca-Cola polar bear scenes to complete. Especially popular at Christmas, look for them in markets, retail stores, chain stores and gift shops for $15–25.

Be on the lookout for puzzles manufactured by Warren Industries. In 1998 Warren issued a hundred-piece puzzle in a box with polar bears participating in various sports. The same images were duplicated in fifty-piece mini-puzzles. Recycled paper is used in both editions.

Another major puzzle manufacturer, the AMG Corp, combined two puzzles (Puz and Puz Jr) in one canister, in 1997. This thousand-piece adult version and thirty-six-piece edition for children showed a cub holding a red beach ball with white stars and a seal offering to share his bottle of Coke. An Arctic night and star-filled sky provided the background.

The following year, AMG released a thousand-piece puzzle packaged in a decorator tin. The puzzle and tin depict a chess game between the bear cubs with adult bear looking on. All three bears are drinking Cokes, and their seal friend is pushing a cooler full of Coke bottles in the water just off the ice floe. A bonus dancing cub magnet is attached to the top of the tin.

One of the more unusual puzzles comes in a tin picturing three different winter sports bears in separate panels. The tin declares it "solves the broken (puzzle) box problem."

School Supplies

Stuart Hall, a major supplier of stationery and school supplies, has produced several lines of notebooks, binders, folders, diaries, date books, schedulers and other school supplies featuring a variety of polar bear poses, including Attitude Bear.

Pentech makes pens and pencils with accessories. A line of Coca-Cola roller ball pens comes in a matching collector's tin with the polar bear logo. One imaginative pen holds ten spring-loaded pen tips of different colored ink. The polar bear turns to pull the color tip back into the pen. A decal on the pen shows a space ship full of polar bears in bubble helmets floating toward the stars.

Xonex, known for die-cast pedal cars, also makes a six pack of Coke cans containing art supplies that feature the polar bear. Each Coke can must be opened to find stamps, ink pad, color pencils, chalk, watercolors, paint brush, pencils, erasers and sharpeners. It retails for

$15. Xonex also makes a pack of jumbo crayons for $10 that has a polar bear family on the box.

Office supply, retail chain, drug and variety stores may all carry these items. Grocery stores and office supply shops are good sources, especially during back-to-school sales.

Snowglobes

CGI has created many intriguing snowglobes to delight the young and young-at-heart alike. Snowglobes may also contain musical movements. "Coca-Cola Polar Bear with Snowshoes," made in 1994, was the first to feature bears and plays "I'd Like to Buy the World a Coke."

The Heritage Gift collection has featured several polar bear snowglobes that are very collectible and reasonably priced, between $40–60.

Cavanagh Heritage Line Snowglobes

Year	Title/Description	Item#
1994	"Coca-Cola Polar Bear" single bear on ice base	H32001
1995	"Refreshing the Slopes" skiing bear on ice base	H32008
	"Santa and Polar Bear"	H73004
1996	"Kids Wrestling" cubs playing on ice base	H73001
1997	"Hollywood" resting against North Pole	H73002
1999	"Perfect Refreshment" polar bear and penguin	HC0202
	"Special Treat" polar bear at soda fountain	HC0203
2000	Bear in green delivery truck	HC0207
	Polar diner	HC0209
	Bear with dancing cubs	HC0210

Stationery

Notepads, cards,
postcards, letter
paper, envelopes,
calendars—the
list goes on and
on for polar bear
stationery items. Try
stationers, craft, gift and
collectible stores for these items. Stuart
Hall is a leading manufacturer of
Coca-Cola Polar Bear
stationery.

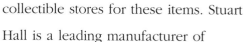

Stickers

Stickers never seem to go out of style, and editions featuring Coca-Cola
polar bears can be found at discount, drug and variety stores across the
country. Here are some favorites:

A page of ten 1997 Coca-Cola holiday stickers featured either a
bottle of Coke or the words "Enjoy Coca-Cola" on whimsical scenes of
a penguin pulling a sled of ice blocks, balancing a bottle on his nose
or pleading for a taste of Coke. Other stickers in the set showed a cub's

ice skating spill, a cub sledding on a bottle cap and a rare appearance of adult bears with cub riding on a toboggan and carrying a case of Coke. The largest sticker pictures a cub standing on an upside-down seal about to place a star atop a very green Christmas tree. Many Christmas cards and gifts were decorated with these stickers by Coca-Cola and polar bear lovers.

In 1998, the Mello Smello Company introduced all kinds of stickers often found in gumball machines. These Coca-Cola polar bear stickers come in many sizes and shapes (round, square, oblong, die cut). Several sparkle with glitter (prismatic). Some of these same scenes are produced as temporary tattoos.

Some of the sticker artwork has not been seen before: a cub holding a Coke bottle in a salute against a pastel-colored sky; a bear with a bottle wearing sun glasses and leaning on a giant bottle of Coke; an adult bear referee and two cub soccer players celebrating victory in front of the net; adult bear and cubs catching a large bottle of Coke through the ice; a big bear on a Coca-Cola motorcycle; and a bear holding a Coke bottle wearing skates, a helmet and knee guards that sport the dynamic swirl.

Collectors also can hunt for a 1998 Collector's Sticker book featuring more than a hundred stickers and a bonus prismatic sticker. Or a Magic Clings by Mello Smello that store stickers on a removable page. Magic Cling window border, centerpieces, mobiles, and luminaries are available from all kinds of toy, gift, stationery and retail stores.

And in case you haven't found just the right sticker, try Smilemakers for rolls of round polar bear stick-anywhere images.

Sun Catchers

Sunbelt Marketing offers hand-painted glass sun catchers in varied sizes and shapes.

Several designs feature polar bears painted in dazzling white and ranging from $9–18 in price. Some designs also appear as nightlights for $15 each.

Tins

The Tin Box Company offers polar bear collectors editions in a variety of shapes and sizes. Tin boxes come in oval, round, square, heart, eyeglass and pencil shapes, as lunchboxes— really everything you could want with polar bears easily accessible through retailers across the country.

Popcorn tins, most plentiful at Christmastime, have been decorated in various polar bear themes, including sports and family scenes. The tins, filled with any number of varieties of popcorn, make great holiday gifts.

Telephones

Coca-Cola polar bears also appear on telephones. One dark blue model from Kash n' Gold LTD can switch between pulse and tone mode. In addition to the adult bear holding a bottle, the "Always Coca-Cola" with bottle disc appeared twice.

Where there are phones, could polar bear phone cards be far behind? At least two dozen have been manufactured in America and abroad during the phone card craze in the 1990s.

Thermometers

Thermometers have served as popular advertising pieces for Coca-Cola since the 1920s. It seems fair that polar bears would eventually stake their claim to this category. An adult bear holds a Coke in a winter scene on a 1994 round plastic thermometer. While it seems that readings of "cold, colder, and coldest" should be suffi-cient for that part of the country, it registers both Cel-sius and Fahrenheit readings. A red Coca-Cola disc with bottle anchors the scale.

Tote Bags

What better way to carry all your favorite polar bear items with you than a Coca-Cola polar bear tote bag? Collectors love this blue-and-white-striped canvas tote bag with a bear and bottle vinyl silhouette stitched into the canvas. Introduced in 1997, it may still be found in the luggage or handbag sections of many discount houses.

Toy Cars and Trucks

Matchbox has produced several toy cars and trucks featuring Coca-Cola polar bears. Another manufacturer of die-cast cars and semi-trucks is Majorette. Prices range from $10–50 at toy stores, collectible shops, discount stores and retail chains. Ertl Collectibles manufactures a 1/64 scale Coca-Cola polar bear ski scene on a tractor trailer for $40–45.

A 1/64 scale Winross tanker truck was authorized for exclusive distribution by The Coca-Cola Collectors Club at its twenty-second annual convention in 1996 in Reston, Virginia. The artwork was developed by a club member and specified only for that event.

Toy Train Sets

From Ertl Collectibles comes a whimsical three-piece metal train with a polar bear train engineer and caboose full of cubs, while a penguin rides herd on two cases of bottles on a flat car. The train sells for $20–25.

A pewter six-car train set, made in 1995, uniquely combines several Coke advertising themes. Each symbol, including an ice cube, the hot sun, the "Always Coca-Cola" disc, a Coke bottle, a Coke bottle cap and a Coca-Cola polar bear, rides in its own individual car. This 9-1/2 inch by 1-1/2 inch collectible is valued at $40–50.

In 1998, The Danbury Mint released a colorful six-car cast metal Christmas train. Santa rides in the engine while a polar bear with shovel sits astride the coal car. Three penguins ride a flat car filled with Coca-Cola barrels and two more penguins hold on to a tanker car. Cubs decorate a Christmas tree in another flat car filled with presents

and a case of Coke. And a polar bear waves from the back of the caboose. All of the figures hold a bottle of their favorite drink.

Another 1998 train set was released by Revell: a 1/64 die cast of the Coca-Cola Dale Earnhardt/Dale Earnhardt Jr. Tribute Train. The set includes seven pieces—five train cars and two car models (on flatbeds)—all black except for the Dale Earnhardt Jr. No. 1 red Monte Carlo. The train cars are decorated with combinations of the black-and-white-checkered bottle on red disc, the polar bear in one of two poses, the NASCAR logo and signatures of the drivers.

A large HO scale train car bearing the face of a polar bear is made for serious train collectors and retails for $150–175.

Trays and Signs

For all the Coca-Cola trays, coasters, tip trays and signs produced through the years, very few have featured polar bears. The first tray was issued in 1993 when the Coca-Cola polar bear was introduced to the public. Made of steel, this tray is 10-1/2 inches by 13 inches and is entitled "Always Cool," picturing an adult bear, a bottle of Coke and the Always red disc. It has been issued in both a round and rectangular shape.

What polar bear lover could resist the round tray on the next page with adult bear and cubs holding their favorite refreshment? It will always be a favorite!

Other polar bear trays include the Skiing Bear, bear outside an igloo, bear with Santa, Adult Bear with cub and sports bears.

Two of the most unusual trays issued to date include a blue serving tray with handles showing the community of bears watching the Northern Lights, anda rounded bowl-shaped tray with three-dimensional figures (a bear and Santa) on the rim.

Wallcovering

Perfect for the polar bear fanatic. Now you can border your bedroom walls with those famous Coca-Cola icons. This border paper comes in a standard double roll with three scenes: adult bear with cubs selling Coke at their neighborhood stand, two cubs skating, and five adults in a group watching. This paper, made by Village Wallcovering, is seven inches wide.

Yo-Yos

Got a kid who's into yo-yos? Considering the large number of these special editions sold every year, it is clear yo-yos aren't just children's toys anymore. Some collectors specialize in just polar bear yo-yos.

Zzzzz

And that's not to mention the thousands of items featuring the favorite polar bears—fan pulls, golf club covers, lava lamps, lead crystal bears with cubs, license plates, pool cues, posters, pot holders, bear-shaped sports bottles, thimbles, toys, watch fobs, wind socks, wrought iron hooks . . . .

And the list goes on and on and on. Everything a polar bear collector could ask for.

CHAPTER 5

Preserving and Displaying Your Collection

Now that you have a pretty good idea what kinds of Coca-Cola polar bear items are available, you probably will want to build or expand your collection. But, then again, you probably didn't need a book to tell you that collecting Coca-Cola polar bears is habit-forming.

It all starts with just one item, then the collection grows and grows until the inevitable question arises: What do you do with all this stuff?

First and foremost, if you're an avid collector, you'll want to leave all items in their original packaging to maintain optimum value. But there are plenty of other considerations when it comes to preserving or displaying your ever-growing investment.

Since Coca-Cola polar bears adorn virtually every collectible imaginable, we'll cover preservation, storage, insurance options and display for several major types of collectibles.

All Collectibles

Think acid-free. In its natural state the tree, from which paperboard is produced, absorbs numerous chemicals from the air and ground and is highly acidic by nature. Untreated paper pulp, made from wood pulp, is therefore acidic as well. The acid in untreated paperboard tends to leach the color out of objects it comes in contact with.

We have experienced this color degradation in old newspapers and our old family photo albums with faded and yellow photos. This inherent acid also accelerates deterioration of the paper itself. We have all noticed old papers and boxes stored in our attics become brittle and have a tendency to fall apart.

Extreme temperatures and high humidity accelerate the destructive effect of acid on your collectibles. Temperatures above 80 and below 50 degrees represent potential hazards for the paint on many collectibles. The expansion and contraction of the paint on a daily basis, in an attic, for example, will tend to cause microscopic cracks in painted surfaces.

These cracks weaken the bond with the paint and destroy the continuity of the surface, allowing for penetration of harmful airborne chemicals in the environment that accelerate the aging of your collectibles.

Humidity above sixty percent represents a humid condition. The humid air carries numerous chemicals with it, which can deteriorate your collectibles. Some of the more common forms of moisture deterioration are rust, corrosion, mold and mildew.

Shifting your display helps protect against long-term direct sunlight that will fade color. In general, keep all collectibles away from the sun.

Some collectors use cotton gloves when they handle unpackaged or loose vintage and prized pieces. Always wash your hands thoroughly, preferably with an oil-free soap, before touching your collectibles with your bare hands.

Animation Cels

The best way to display your cels, and keep them protected, is by framing them. Framers may use regular glass, den (or museum) glass or plexiglass.

Plexiglass is lightweight and durable but can promote static electricity which could pull or bend your image. Den glass is less reflective and filters out many of the sun's rays but can be more expensive.

If framing is not an option, you may try storing your cels in mylar sleeves or art portfolios. If you plan to stack cels on top of one another, you may wish to matte them first to keep separation and distribute the weight.

Avoid dust, of course, but compressed air can clean most dusty cels if needed. Heavy dirt, tape marks, etc., can often be cleaned with a cotton swab dipped in rubbing alcohol, but be careful not to touch painted areas.

If you don't trust your cleaning skills, seek the help of a professional restorer. Although animation cels may cost more to restore than other types of art, a restorer can solve many problems such as cracked paint.

Cans and Bottles

Some collectors prefer to collect full cans and bottles, but be aware of the potential hazards. Full cans and bottles are heavier, making display trickier, and some cans tend to leak after just a year.

Simple dusting will keep your cans and bottles looking like new.

Figurines

Most figurines can be maintained by regular gentle dusting with a feather duster, paint brush or compressed air. Figurines also can be bathed using lukewarm water and mild dish soap, if needed. Be sure to thoroughly rinse all soap residue from the figurine to keep it from attracting more dust once it has dried.

Ornaments

Unlike other pieces in a collection, ornaments often spend more time in storage than on display. For this reason, it's important to store ornaments in rigid boxes with compartments or dividers to avoid the pieces touching one another. Acid-free cardboard boxes are preferred. Hard plastic storage boxes can trap moisture, and many plastics contain harmful chemicals.

For packing materials, choose acid-free tissue or paper towels or one hundred percent cotton fabric.

Newspaper and bubble wrap are not recommended for storing your keepsakes.

As mentioned earlier, humidity and temperature are your enemy, so household closets, cupboards and drawers are preferred over garages, attics and basements.

Plates

The same rules used for figurines also apply for plates. When washing your plates use a mild soap and thoroughly rinse and dry. Do not place collectible plates in the dishwasher or use to serve food.

Small easels are popular for displaying individual plates. Wood and plastic frames, made especially for plates, also exist and range from $15–25.

Plush

Dirt and smudges can be tricky when dealing with plush and bean bags. If necessary, take a small amount of non-scented liquid soap and water and put it on a towel. Then gently rub the soapy part of the towel on the dirty spot. Never machine wash any of the bean bag toys. The companies simply don't recommend it.

Several types of tag protectors are available, including ones that clip around the tags and others that slide over them.

Many versions of standard plastic display cases also exist. But if you want to tuck some away for prosperity, you may want to do so in a zipper-style plastic bag, especially if there's a smoker in the house. Smoke may find its way into a plastic case or curio cabinet, but not a good bag.

Display options abound with Coca-Cola bean bags and plush,

thanks to an array of accessories produced by Cavanagh Group International. Cavanagh produces everything from sleighs and sling chairs to benches and bicycles.

Insuring Your Collection

No matter how big or small the size of your collection, you should consider insuring your valuables in case of theft, fire, flood or any other kind of destruction. Cherished collectibles usually can't be replaced in the heart, but that doesn't mean the disaster has to be an entire loss.

Collectors often can get a new lease on life if they have had the proper insurance on their collection. A well-funded collector can get right back in the hunt, often with a much better idea of chasing down all those items on the new want list.

Obtaining insurance on your collection isn't difficult, especially if you keep your collectibles at your home. Talk to your agent about the specifics of your collection. In many cases, a small collection will already be covered under your current homeowners insurance. But the bigger and more valuable the collection, the more insurance you'll need.

Many policies insure specific categories of items, such as a toy car and truck collection, only up to a certain amount. If your collection's value is above that amount, you can "schedule" out specific items and insure those separately. Some companies even offer special collector's insurance that requires a professional appraisal. If your collection is big enough, going through this process can be well worth it. Even if you have to get an addendum or rider added to your current policy, it is easily done and affordable.

Renters who keep their collection at home should make sure they have renter's insurance.

Collectors should keep accurate records of their collection, including purchase prices and receipts. In addition, maintain an inventory checklist and photograph your collection. Keep these in a safe place, away from the collection, so that you will have your records if disaster strikes.

Resources

The Coca-Cola Company, Atlanta, Georgia

http://www.coca-cola.com

Appendix A

Following are companies that manufacture Coca-Cola licensed products containing polar bears, as of the publication of this book. These companies DO NOT sell directly to consumers. Ask your local stores if they carry these lines or can order them for you. Most products are available only for one season, then retired. Many manufacturers are represented by companies who market their products to retailers in various parts of the country.

Action Performance Corporation

Phoenix, Arizona

http://home.action-performance.com

Die-cast vehicles, helmets, gas pumps, lead crystal cars

AMG Corp

Puzzles

Aminco

Irvine, California

www.amincousa.com

Pins, key chains, magnets

Ansco
    Elk Grove Village, Illinois
    www.anscophoto.com
    Cameras

Arjon Manufacturing
    Maplewood, New Jersey
    www.arjon.com
    Magnets

Bicycle Company (see United States Playing Card Company)
    Cincinnati Ohio
    Playing cards

Buckles of America
    Americraft Pewter Accessories
    Rocklin, California
    www.apapewter.com
    Pewter ware, key chains, magnets, pins

Buztronics, Inc.
    Indianapolis, Indiana
    www.buztronics.com
    Flashing balls

Cavanagh Group International (CGI),
    Alpharetta, Georgia
    www.cavanaghgrp.com
    Clocks, cookie jars, figurines, jewelry, mugs, musicals, ornaments,
    photo frames, snowglobes, plush

Classico of California
    Corte Madera, California
    www.classicosanfrancisco.com
    Postcards, Christmas cards

Computer Expressions
    Philadelphia, Pennsylvania
    www.compexpress.com/LineFhtml/CokeF.html
    Mousepads

Enesco Corporation
    Itasca, Illinois
    www.enesco.com
    Banks, dishes, figurines, musicals

Ertl Collectibles
    Dyersville, Iowa
    www.ertltoys.com
    Banks, die-cast vehicles, toy cars and trucks, trains

General Time Corporation (Westclox)
    Norcross, Georgia
    www.westclox.com
    Clocks, key chains, watches

Gift Creations
    Chatsworth, California
    www.giftcreations.com
    Key chains, pins, frames, mugs

Indiana Glass
    Cincinnati, Ohio
    Glasses, glass platters

Jaygur Imports
    Montreal, Canada
    www.jaygur.com
    Backpacks, knapsacks

Kurt Adler
    New York, New York
    www.kurtadler.com

Majorette
    Solido
    Miami, Florida
    www.majorette.com
    Toy cars and trucks

Matchbox
    Mattel, Inc.
    El Segundo, California
    www.matchboxtoys.com
    Toy cars and trucks

Mattel Corporation
    Mattel, Inc.
    El Segundo, California
    www.barbie.com
    Barbie

Mello Smello
    Minneapolis, Minnesota
    www.mellosmello.com
    Greeting cards, stickers, luminaries

Midwest of Cannon Falls, Incorporated
    Cannon Falls, Minnesota
    www.midwestofcannonfalls.com
    Porcelain boxes

Monogram International
    Largo, Florida
    www.monintl.com
    Pins, keyrings, banks, magnets

Name That Toon Company
    San Rafael, California
    www.namethattoon.com
    Animation Cels

Pentech
    Edison, New Jersey
    www.wshowcase.com/pentech
    Pens, pencils, pen tins

Revell
    Mortongrove, Illinois
    www.revell-monogram.com
    Die-cast vehicles, train sets

Shadle Enterprises
    Atlanta, Georgia
    Signs, license plates, waste baskets

Sunbelt Marketing
    North Charleston, South Carolina
    Suncatchers, nightlights, gold bottles

Stuart Hall
    Pen-Tab Industries
    Front Royal, Virginia
    www.stuarthall.com
    School supplies, date books, address books, diaries, stationery

Tin Box Company
    Farmingdale, New York
    www.tinboxco.com
    Tins, metal cases, lunch boxes

Trademark Marketing
    Alpharetta, Georgia
    Trays, tins

Warren Industries
    www.wrnind.com
    Puzzles

United States Playing Card Company
    Cincinnati, Ohio
    www.usplayingcard.com
    Playing cards

Village Wallcovering
   Cranbury, New Jersey
   Wallpaper

Xonex
   Cleveland, Ohio
   www.xonexintl.com
   Die-cast, school supplies

Appendix B

Companies that sell directly to consumers or have a website where you can order products.

Always Collectors Corner
   www.4beanies-cola.com/polarbears.html
   Site with updated Coca-Cola polar bear products and resources

Beckett Publications
   15850 Dallas Parkway
   Dallas, TX 75248
   www.beckett.com
   Books (*Coca-Cola Collectible Bean Bags & Plush*)

Cavanagh Coca-Cola Collectors Society
   P.O. Box 768090
   Roswell, GA 30076
   www.cavanaghgrp.com
   800-653-1221
   Members-only figurines, bean bags

Coca-Cola Pin Catalog
   PO Box 182264
   Chattanooga, TN 37422
   800-265-3746
   Pins, framed pin sets

Coca-Cola Store
   www.coca-colastore.com
   1-800-Shop-Coke
   Everything Coca-Cola

Danbury Mint
   47 Richards Ave.
   Norwalk, CT 06857
   www.danburymint.com
   1-800-243-4664
   Toy trains, Steiff Polar Bear

Franklin Mint
   www.franklinmint.com
   Collector plates, figurines, musicals

Name-That-Toon Company
   28 Mountain View Ave.
   San Rafael, CA 94901
   www.namethattoon.com
   Animation Cels

Smilemakers
   www.smilemakers.com
   1-800-825-8085
   Stickers

World of Coca-Cola stores
   Atlanta   800-676-2653
   Las Vegas   800-720-2653
   Atlanta Airport 404-763-3166

The
Coca-Cola
Collectors
Club

In 1974, Bob Buffaloe, of Memphis, Tennessee, ran an advertisement to see if there were any other collectors of The Coca-Cola Company's memorabilia interested in forming a club. As a result of this ad, The "Cola Clan" was organized, and out of this organization grew The Coca-Cola Collectors Club. The first newsletter was mailed to fifty-two members in January 1975, and the first convention was held in Atlanta, Georgia, in August 1975 with twenty-four attendees. In August 1999, the twenty-fifth convention was held in Dallas, Texas, with an attendance of more than sixteen hundred.

The Coca-Cola Collectors Club is a non-profit organization for collectors and their families who are interested in the history of The Coca-Cola Company and anything featuring the Coca-Cola and Coke trademarks. Since the club's early beginnings, it has grown to more than five thousand members in North America alone, with several hundred more members located throughout the rest of the world. The Coca-Cola Collectors Club still publishes a monthly newsletter providing members with information on collecting, club activities, classified ads and member merchandise specials.

The club holds a yearly convention where members gather to learn more about Coca-Cola collecting, to buy, sell and trade items, and meet and greet old friends. In addition, there are more than fifty local chapters, most of which hold regular meetings, print newsletters and host regional conventions that attract up to a thousand attendees. With the help of The Coca-Cola Collectors Club you can find out about something for the Coca-Cola collector in every part of the world, in every month of the year.

For further information or to join write:

The Coca-Cola Collectors Club

PMB 609

4780 Ashford Dunwoody Rd, Suite A

Atlanta, Georgia 30338

Coca-Cola Collectors Club Website:

www.cocacolaclub.org

The Coca-Cola Collectors Club is run by unpaid volunteers elected by the membership and is not sponsored by The Coca-Cola Company.

About the Authors

Linda Lee Harry

Linda spent several years working in mission hospitals in Korea and Thailand, collecting Coca-Cola bottles from the many places she visited. Then, while working in a hospital lab in Oregon, she was chemically poisoned, severely damaging her immune system. Friends brought Coke bottles from around the world to brighten long hospital stays in isolation.

Soon, Linda's collection filled several rooms. Collecting Coca-Cola memorabilia became the family hobby and respite through many difficult years of recovery. When times were hard, Linda reluctantly sold some of the collection. Her sister, Suzi Harry, built a website (Always Collectors Corner) to show Linda's unique Coca-Cola pieces. The site remains today, carrying a full line of Coca-Cola collectibles and specialty bean bag plush.

Jean Gibbs-Simpson

A native of Kansas, Jean Gibbs-Simpson lives in Lawrence with her husband, Ed Simpson. She is a retired college registrar and church treasurer.

After collecting any and all Coca-Cola memorabilia for twenty-five years, Jean turned her focus to the polar bears in 1993 when the first polar bear ad was shown on television.

Since Jean began collecting in the 1970s, she also has been a member of The Coca-Cola Collectors Club where she's served in most of the executive board positions, including president and publications director.

She currently serves as membership director. Also instrumental in the founding of the Mid-America chapter of the club, based in Kansas City, Jean edited the chapter's newsletter for several years and coordinated two national conventions.

Jean and Ed do not see their collecting passion waning anytime soon, nor do they intend to give up the camaraderie and friendships that exist among active collectors.

Acknowledgments

The authors and editors of this book wish to thank the following people and companies for their generosity: Tony Tortorici, Ed Simpson, Suzi Harry, Sandra Silvius, Scott Byrd, David Zimmerman, Judith Miller, Sherry McCullough, Margaret Harry, William Paul, Jim Hollister, Kathy Scales, John Cavanagh, Dee Dukes, Karleen Buchholtz, Rhythm & Hues, FAO Schwarz, Steiff, Cavanagh Group International and the Lone Star chapter of the Coca-Cola Collectors Club.

PHOTOGRAPHY

"Polar Bear Concept" photos courtesy of Rhythm & Hues

Polar bear plush photos pp. 8, 43–44, 49, 51–54, 56–59 are
   courtesy of Cavanagh Group International.

All other photography by Mark Delich, Zoom Studio

BOOK DESIGN

Book format design by Sara Maneval

Layout by Hespenheide Design